The Millionaire Trader Compilation

Cameron Lancaster

Table of Contents

Introduction 7

How to Reduce Your Trading Costs 12

Market Efficiency? A Statistical Look 20

The Anatomy of a Stock Bubble 32

Leverage, Carry Trades, and Beta 39

Long Term Return Forecast by Sector 48

How to Use Tax Loss Harvesting to Beat the Market 50

Closing 54

Understand The (Actual) Basics Of Options 57

Understand Volatility and Put/Call Parity 74

Know the Expected Value of Options Contracts 82

How to Size Your Trades: John Kelly vs. John Daly 90

Where to Find Trading Ideas 97

Why Most Options Traders Lose Money 100

Bonus Tips on Trading 103

Is the Stock Market the Best Place to Invest? 110

The Wide World of Investments 114

Real Estate 119
Peer to Peer Investment 133
Semi-Absentee Businesses 145
Closing Thoughts- The Millionaire Trader Compilation 156

Publishers Note:

This is a compilation of the Millionaire Trader series books by Cameron Lancaster. We have compiled the set and offered it at a nice discount to buying all three books. Note that the content is the same from each book previously published.

Each book occupies a niche that helps a different kind of investor achieve their goals. *How to Beat the Market* is Mr. Lancaster's advice on stock investing using solid, research based methods to achieve superior returns. *How to Make a Million Dollars Trading Options* is an edited and repackaged compilation of a series of emails between Mr. Lancaster and a multimillionaire options trader. *The Passive Income Playbook* offers advice on alternative investments, which we believe offer a better risk/reward for a sizeable minority of investors.

Each book offers a different approach to building wealth through investing and trading. While the approaches are different, the methods outlined in each book are all backed by decades of research and have strong expected and prior returns. By presenting all three approaches we hope that you find the best solution for you.

How to Beat the Market: Stock Market Tips for Your First 1,000,000

Copyright © 2017 Lancaster Chatham Publishing

Introduction

Is it possible to beat the market? Naysayers will say that the stock market is fully efficient and that you can't beat the market. They usually are just bad at investing and think everyone else is too. **You can beat the market, and you can beat it handily. Wall Street pros have been doing it under the radar for decades with simple, easy to understand investment strategies.**

Don't listen to people who can't make money in the stock market and never will. Your hard earned cash deserves better than incompetent financial advisors and fee hungry stockbrokers. Use the tactics in this book to make your investments grow faster! Everything is explained in plain English, not in technical mumbo-jumbo.

Inside:

How Robinhood and Interactive Brokers make it easier to beat the market.

Breaking down the myth of market efficiency.

How to profit from market bubbles and avoid the burst!

A brief introduction to smart beta

How to use carry trades and leverage (when appropriate).

Return forecast by sector.

How to get a free lunch with tax loss harvesting software, and much more.

Talking heads on television are eager to tell you that it is impossible to beat the S&P 500 average. They say that your best option is to reduce your investment selection process down to just buying one S&P 500 mutual fund and forgetting about it. Perhaps they themselves tried to beat the market but lost money. They're missing the point though. Stock returns aren't random. You can beat the market! You just have to think about it a little differently. Start by listening to people who can help you think through problems and find solutions, not those who just throw up their hands and say beating the market is impossible. These are literally the same people who will tell you that you can't make over 100k a year because most people don't. Well, that's shitty but that just means they can't make 100k per year, not that no one can. I have news for you. People make millions of dollars trading on Wall Street Every. Single. Day. Sometimes these same people get hit with margin calls, but the amount of OPM involved on Wall Street is mind blowing. Take a look sometime at Dennis Connor Marina in Manhattan. There are a bunch of yachts there, and it costs an outrageous amount for the privilege of parking your yacht there. Do you want that? Or do you want to have a stable income in retirement? This is a yacht party in NYC kind of book.

Why would you want to take advice from someone who can't even begin to think about beating the market?

If it is very possible to systematically lose money in the stock market, it is equally possible to be smart and systematically make money, even in excess of the S&P 500's return. It's time to take responsibility for your investments. If you're doing well, then great! You might be able to do even better but what you are doing is working. If you're doing okay or poorly, then you should be open to making some changes. As you will see, learning some of the mechanics of how stock returns work is key to improving returns. I will show you some easy methods that will help improve your performance in the market, and hopefully will give you some specific, actionable knowledge you can use to make more money and beat the market.

How to Reduce Your Trading Costs

First and foremost, playing the market is a business, and commissions, fees, bid/ask spreads, and interest are your costs. You can't run a profitable business if you overpay all your suppliers, and you can't run a profitable portfolio if you pay over the bare minimum in commissions, interest and fees. The higher volume of trades you make, the more apparent it is that trading is a volume business and that small edges add up to huge numbers given enough time. Commissions are like cancer to your trading account. They eat away at your profit relentlessly. *Rule number one in business is to control costs.* Like Matthew McConaughey tells Leonardo DiCaprio in Wolf of Wall Street, the brokers' goal is to keep the clients on the train, feeding them new ideas that they make and lose large amounts of cash on, so they don't notice the steady stream of cash flowing out the door in commissions. This is true for online brokers, human stockbrokers and basically everyone involved in stocks. The commission goes out the door in cold, hard cash, and the client profits all happen on paper.

The TV gurus are halfway right, because they warn about the risks of overtrading. If you trade too much without an edge, you will lose money to the steady grind of commissions, and guys like Leonardo and Matthew's characters will get your money to spend on Quaaludes and crazy women. The solution here, if you are a trader, is to use a lower cost broker to trade instead of high cost brokers like Etrade. Robinhood is 100 percent free, but their current 50,000-dollar per day deposit limit indicates that they don't want to service a lot of multimillionaire clients. They also don't support options currently, but they if they do in the future, things could get very interesting. There is no reason not to use Robinhood for your trading if it doesn't cramp your trading goals. If it does, switch to the next best choice. The next best choice is Interactive brokers, especially for active traders, even though they charge a dollar per trade, it is 85 percent lower than their competitors. Interactive

Brokers is where serious traders trade, the kind of people who make a living from trading trade there. They have everything that active traders need, such as options, cheap margin, low fees, and lightning fast execution. Robinhood isn't the fastest on the execution, so it really depends on whether you day trade or hold on to your investments for a while. The bottom line is that commissions are a problem, and you want to reduce them or you will prove the gurus right when they beat you with their index funds. This example should help you see how much fees add up.

On average, active traders make a few trades per week, which is not many compared to the dozens of trades day traders can make on a daily basis. Picture a 50,000-dollar portfolio of a trader who makes 5 round trip trades on average, per week, for a total of 10 trades per week (5 buys, 5 sells).

Broker charging 7 dollars per trade=70 dollars per week, 280 dollars per month, 3,360 dollars per year. This amounts to roughly a 6.7 percent house edge against the trader over the course of a year. This is only a typical example; heavy traders can easily triple that number without breaking a sweat. Assuming that each trade is made with 20,000 dollars of the 50,000, which is fair, because you don't want every single dime on the line on each trade, this is a 0.07 percent edge in favor of the house on each trade. It is amazing how 0.07 percent per trade adds up to a 6.7 percent edge in favor of the house over the course of a year. The difference is that the commissions have no benefit to you, and your total cost can only go up, not down. That means that every good trade you make, your broker makes 14 bucks. (7 on the buy, 7 on the sell). Every okay trade you make, they make 14 bucks. Every bad trade you make, guess what, they also make 14 bucks. It adds up folks. The more you trade, the more this effect is exaggerated.

Let's rerun the same example with Interactive Brokers, which charges 1 dollar per trade.

Broker charging 1 dollar per trade=10 dollars per week, 40 dollars per month, 480 dollars per year

Day Traders will make thousands of trades per year. Don't start your trading by bleeding tens of thousands of dollars in commissions, it makes it harder to compound the wins. And that, folks, is the difference between supporting your broker being able to afford cocaine and your broker drinking cheap liquor. You'll never meet your online broker so cheap liquor for them all the way! Your responsibility to your bank account and net worth is to select a broker that will charge less.

Market Efficiency? A Statistical Look

The first step to understand what market efficiency really means is to understand where stock returns come from. Let's say the S&P 500 returned 10 percent last year. Of the 500 stocks, let's say a few went down a ton, a few stocks broke even, a lot of stocks went up a little, a few went up more than the market, and a few stocks had huge gains. Knowing that a few stocks are responsible for a lot of the returns in the market, you have to wonder if you could predict them ahead of time. Proponents of market efficiency would argue that it is impossible to predict with any accuracy which stocks will go up more than the market. I think they have a good point, but you can identify which stocks have a lot of potential to go up, the same way a tornado watch can show where there is a lot of potential for tornados.

Best performing S&P 500 stocks, 2016

NVDA +227 percent

OKE +150 percent

FCX +95 percent

NEM +90 percent

SE +80 percent

AMAT +76 percent

PWR +72 percent

CMA +66 percent

MLM +64 percent

HAL +62 percent

All of these stocks have one of two things in common. They are either in technology, or are in industries that are very cyclical. This shows to me, that if you want to pick stocks and beat the market, you should focus on cyclical stocks that are undervalued, just like Benjamin Graham or Warren Buffett would, or should invest in technology.

I won't list the 10 worst companies in the S&P 500 for last year, but they also have some things in common. They biggest thing that they have in common is debt that they can't pay and losing money. That is the number one way to avoid losers is to not invest in companies that lose money. It sounds so simple but people fail to do this all the time and invest in companies that do nothing but light their cash on fire. The good news is that stocks can only go to zero, and they can go up huge.

Another interesting tidbit is that NVDA was one of the best performers in 2015 also, so sometimes you can't argue against success. This is actually an interesting argument for diversification, because one NVDA can make up for 3 busts, since the stock more than tripled in one year. A hidden drawback to index funds is that they are weighted by market cap, meaning that you can't get huge exposure to a stock like NVDA and have a lot of your eggs riding in the basket of a few stocks. That said, it is easy to correct for this flaw by mixing and matching index funds (Vanguard has tons of good index funds) to make a balanced portfolio. You deserve better than the return of the S&P 500, and whether you choose to get your upside from picking stocks or weighting different Vanguard funds, you will increase your return and reduce your risk.

So, the first thing you need to do is to identify stocks and sectors with the potential for growth. This is much easier than it sounds! For example, technology has an expected earnings growth rate sector wide of roughly double what utilities have. PWR is a construction firm by the way, not a utility. Mark my words, you will never find a public utility on the best performing stock list. There just simply isn't enough potential for growth. You want the kind of stocks where effort can make a difference. Utilities are 2D, whereas technology is 3D.

The other type of stock perpetually on the best performer list is cyclical companies. Here, if you have the ability to do the handicapping to make sure that the company won't literally run out of money, you can buy stocks 50+ percent off when the cycle is at the bottom and double your money when the cycle turns. Macro hedge funds make a living doing this sort of thing in cyclical companies. The main risk you face here is buying too early. To avoid this, you need to understand the supply and demand effects of crude oil especially. Stocks tend to go up after they go down, in a fairly uniform fashion. Down years are followed by up years, based on the valuations of companies. Commodities, which most cyclical industries are, don't work like this. They go off the supply and demand of their underlying markets. The oil market, for example is filled with men with large egos who control the production decisions for a large percentage of global production. They are prone to behaviors such as trying to corner the market, dumping supply on the market to put their competitors out of business, price fixing, etc. This old school capitalism means one thing. *The price of crude has a tendency to crash 80-90 percent, and stay down for a while.* This is due to the people who run the industry. Other commodities suffer from the same swings, although not quite as bad. You can't expect the price to behave rationally, because the suppliers don't behave rationally either. These cycles can take up 24 months to play out, so be patient and don't think things are over when crude is down 25 percent. Because the underlying market is so ridiculous, the stocks tend to also be ridiculous, but tend to lag the crude market by a number of months. Use this to your advantage, and you will have picked some of the best performers in your portfolio. Obviously with these kinds of stocks, you may want to sell them after they have repriced to their fair value so you don't get caught in the next wave.

By now, I'm sure you have heard of the 80/20 rule, which states that 80 percent of your results tend to come from 20 percent of your efforts. Stocks are no different, and I believe over time, that a large share of your profits will come from a small portion of your investments, and a large share of your losses will come from few of your holdings. By identifying which stocks are likely to get hurt and which have potential for large percentage gains, you put yourself ahead of the competition. Markets are mildly efficient, that means that companies don't trade for 1 times earnings for no reason, but human beings have systematic biases that you can exploit to make more profit in stocks. This is how you identify stocks that will do well.

Best Performer Characteristics

- Tend to be in technology or biotechnology
- Tend to have reasonable amounts of debt
- Tend to have big growth potential

Worst Performer Characteristics
- High Debt Levels
- Operate at a loss
- Bad business models- i.e. landline telephones

Don't think about your investments in terms of value vs. growth, that distinction is useless. Think in terms of cash flow and potential growth. This will help sharpen your fundamental analysis skills. The most useless question you can ask is what category a company fits into. Growth, value, etc. all you should care about is making a profit. This goes for market cap too. As long as the market cap is over a microscopic amount (I say 150-200 million is a good floor, just keep smaller companies on the radar unless you really, really believe they have potential), then the company size is not a good reason to invest or not invest. There is no such thing as a company being too big. Big companies tend to get even bigger, and smaller companies are more nimble and have the advantage of being able to turn on a dime. *When investing in big companies, look for those that have the ability to innovate. When investing in small companies, look for their ability to get distribution.*

That determines the winner in a big vs. small matchup in a product market.

Your job as an investor is to find cash flow and growth, and allocate your cash to companies that have these characteristics. Companies make money over time, and this fundamentally is what drives stock prices up. Money flows into the business as profit, where it is used to pay dividends, buy back stock, and grow the business further. Profits also tend to grow over time, producing capital gains as the multiple of the company remains steady. If a company is trading for 10 times earnings and the earnings are steady or rising, then your return should be 10 percent per year, because that is the cash the business throws off. Use some of this type fundamental analysis in your investments; you'd be surprised how few people do! This is how you generate alpha in your investments, beating the other market participants–and the S&P 500.

The Anatomy of a Stock Bubble

"Stock Market just crashed, now I'm just a bill"- Jay Z

Bubbles are the biggest problem for those who believe in market efficiency. In an efficient market, bubbles would not happen. Academics have a variety of explanations that they try to justify bubbles occurring with. I have a simpler equation for them.

Fear + Greed=Asset Bubbles

There are two classic stock market sayings my grandpa used to say. The first is that you make money buying low and selling high (duh), and the other is that there are only two emotions in the stock market, fear and greed. Greed is easy to understand. As a hot market starts to rise, people start to make some nice money. The people who make the most money, compared to their wealth, are those who borrow money from their brokers to invest in stocks. This is the greediest group of people in the stock market, those who max out their margin every chance they get. When you buy stocks on max margin and they go up like 20 percent, you're up 40 percent minus interest because they let you go 2 to 1 leverage. The thing that most people don't know is that when you buy stocks on margin and they go up, you have a higher position value so you can use your new margin created to buy even more stock. **This is called pyramiding.** All speculators do this in one form or another. When they make money, they raise the stakes. What happens if a stock starts going up really fast, you can buy more, and the more it goes up, they more they let you buy. This allows you to lever up like crazy. You can make huge returns on a small amount of money doing this. Note to options traders: you can pyramid with options too; rolling your big options profits into fresh at the money calls after a stock rises. You can make a couple million dollars without breaking a sweat if you do it right, and the odds are much better than you would think. This is called *rolling up and out.* If you catch a big story in a stock, you can watch yourself get rich over a baseball season.

Now the savvy investors among you might be thinking, "Wait a second. Didn't he just tell us to buy low and sell high?" That's right, I did! See the problem with people who use margin isn't that margin is bad, it's that people who use margin tend to suck at investing, and therefore suck at life. Not only do they let you buy more when a stock goes up, but they can force you to sell when it goes down. Ever heard of a margin call? That's what happens when they force you to put up more money to cover a losing margin position, usually when the position value goes down 35-50 percent. So your broker let's you buy more stock at high prices, and forces you to sell or put up more money when the price drops? Yep, that's pretty much how bubbles work. Everyone with a pulse is borrowing money to buy assets when prices are high, and when prices are low, there is no credit to be found and margin calls get issued by the thousand. What happens is stocks go way high, and then a few savvy investors start to take profits, and then a few idiots who are short the stock will plant stories in the media/internet about how the company/market is bad, which might inspire a research downgrade at a big brokerage firm. This feedback causes the stock to sell off more. At this point, people who bought near the top are trying to get out close to even, which puts even more pressure on the stock. Then, maybe some people get margin calls, or maybe they don't, and the smart people who sold at the top start the cycle over again. It isn't the easiest thing in the world to time the market, but it isn't rocket science either.

My point here isn't that margin and pyramiding are horrible, because there is no better way to make a ton of money in a short period of time, but that if you want to use margin, you have to avoid the tendency to buy high and sell low. It takes guts and patience to make money trading on margin! You 100 percent need to be able to have the cash to cover a margin call if you want to trade on margin, and this doesn't mean you sell other stocks to cover a margin call. *You need to have some disposable income if you want to play this game.* Otherwise you are guaranteed to lose. People tend to buy when stocks go up, and they tend to sell when stocks go down. Nothing too complicated here, except that you can lose a lot of money if you follow the herd of lemmings off the cliff. Understand that people tend to panic and sell stocks they don't need to sell, and understand that people tend to buy more of stocks that go up just because they can. They lose a fair amount of money in the process, but that isn't our problem. Just be smart and understand how the process works, and you are miles closer to being one of the smart people who laughs about bubbles rather than the person getting margin calls from their broker.

Leverage, Carry Trades, and Beta

There are two kinds of people in this world. Those who love leverage, and those who hate it. Some of the smartest investors in the world sit on both sides of this debate. If you want to make a bunch of money, though, leverage is your best friend (frenemy). However, despite it's reputation for risky behavior, leverage ratios in stocks tend to be lower than real estate, which I find fascinating. The easiest way to get leverage in stocks, as we discussed before, is to borrow on margin, giving you 2 to 1 leverage on stocks. The two most important things you need for investing on margin are:

1. A low interest rate (IB charges like 2.6 percent at the time of writing)
2. That you can cover a margin call if you need to, i.e. have disposable income.

You might think that since you are paying interest on the margin that you are losing money every day you hold it. This is the biggest check on people going too crazy with leverage, because the interest compounds daily, and is charged out of their accounts on a monthly basis by their brokers. So, most smart traders realize that they shouldn't buy stocks with money they don't have. But, back to the real estate example, investors take mortgages out so they can own a property and rent it out to tenants. No bank will lend to someone who needs to come up with money every month to pay the mortgage, they want a property to cash flow. So, real estate investors might rent an apartment complex out, getting a cap rate of 6-7 percent, pay a fixed mortgage charging them 3-4 percent, and pocket the rest. This is called positive carry. They make money for owning the building. The longer the own the building, the more money they make. Eventually, they cash out when the building appreciates, pay off the mortgage and live happily ever after with their millions in profit. This is the polar opposite of how most people who buy stocks on margin operate. They buy a stock with no dividend, pay to carry it, and panic when it goes down. So, you might see where I'm going here, but if margin rates are like 2 percent and you buy a stock with a dividend of 3 percent, you carry it for free, and if it appreciates, then it's just gravy. Moreover, your dividends, if they are raised, could help pay down the margin interest, which would shrink as the market value rises. This is the basis of the carry trade, and it is how big banks make billions of dollars per year in profit. This is part of the genius of finance, because when you make a positive return carrying an asset, the sky is the limit for how much money you can make. This should have your head spinning with the possibilities.

The carry trade, in its current form started in the mid 1990s in Japan. The stock market bubble burst in Japan, leaving out of control deflation and a sagging economy. In 1995, the central bank of Japan took the unconventional step of setting interest rates at 0.5 percent, where they have stayed at or below since then. At the same time, interest rates in Australia were at 7.5 percent, leaving big traders and banks with some easy, low hanging fruit. All they had to do was borrow yen at 0.5 percent and invest the proceeds in Australian dollars paying 7.5 percent, pocketing a cool 7 percent spread for their trouble. And, given their large amounts of capital, they raked it in. Making the trade even sweeter was the fact that the yen tended to depreciate against other, higher yielding currencies due to the fact that banks were selling it to put their money in places where they could get a yield. Academics struggled to understand how such a simple trade could produce such consistent returns. Traders were levering up, banking 50-60 percent returns year after year. Leverage is a funny thing like that. Academics eventually came up with something called "uncovered interest rate parity," guessing that the currencies with high interest rates would be expected to fall. In practice, actually, currencies with high interest rates from strong countries like the US, UK, and Australia tend to get even stronger when interest rates rise. The only risk to the abnormally high carry trade profits is that a crash might happen which could knock out profit and then some if enough leverage is used. This happened to a lot of people in 2008 when money poured into the yen.

However, the current low interest rate environment in the US has created favorable conditions for a similar carry trade involving stocks. Any stock that has a dividend yield higher than the interest rate at interactive brokers should be considered for a carry trade. As soon as the interest rate climbs above the yield, you sell, walking away with quite a bit of profit. That is how the big boys trade. However, if carry trades aren't your flavor, there are other methods you can use to get more leverage on stocks.

Anytime you get leverage on a stock, you are said to have beta. Beta is defined as the volatility of investments. It is expressed as a positive number, with 1 being the beta of the market. Betas between 0 and 1 are considered less risky than the market as a whole, and numbers greater than 1 are considered more risky. This is the academic view on beta. More standard deviation=more risk=more return. You can get beta from buying volatile stocks, such as the FANG stocks, from buying call options on stocks, or from beta funds. So long as you don't buy high and sell low, leverage (beta) is your best friend.

A buzzword lately in finance is *smart beta,* where instead of taking a market cap weighted position in stocks, the allocation is set by something else, such as price to earnings, volatility or simply equal weights the basket. When you think about it, the decision to weight stocks by market capitalization is somewhat arbitrary, and it stands to reason that an equal weight portfolio could beat the S&P 500 weighted by market cap. This is a unique way to get some extra beta in a way that is beneficial to beating the market. Beta will help you beat the market if you understand how to use it. A word of caution, however, there are some good smart beta funds, and there are some bad ones, so if you choose one for your portfolio use common sense. Look for transparent strategies, low fees, and at least a short track record.

Long Term Return Forecast by Sector

Utilities- 5-6 percent return

Telecom- 5-6 percent return

Materials- 7 percent return

Consumer Discretionary- 8 percent return

Consumer Staples- 8 percent return

Financials- 8 percent return

Energy- 8 percent return

Real Estate- 8 percent return

Health Care- 9 percent return

Technology- 10 percent return

Note: returns are derived from earnings yield, plus my estimate for growth. That is classic discounted cash flow and I think you will find these return assumptions fair and quite accurate over the next decade. Nominal (when you count inflation), US GDP growth is higher than you think at 4-5 percent annually, so use that as your baseline for corporate profits. Growth ranges from 2-3 percent annually for utilities and telecom to 6 percent for technology.

How to Use Tax Loss Harvesting to Beat the Market

Here is a strategy that you can use to beat the market. I don't have to be right for this strategy to work, and you don't have to trust my financial advice. Instead, it just works. As investors, we are trained to buy low and sell high, but for tax purposes, you want to sell at a loss so you can write it off. Basically, how the strategy works is this. For every part of your portfolio, you have two similar but not identical funds to avoid the infamous wash sale rules. Ideally, they will be correlated between 90 and 95 percent, with similar expected return profiles and fee profiles. Any time you have a loss in your portfolio exceeding 1 percent on basis, sell and switch to your other asset. This, for tax purposes, leaves you with losses, while not impacting your actual investment position. Over time, this will defer capital gains and will save you money on your taxes, leaving you with large capital gains that you can take later. The savings generated from tax-loss harvesting can be reinvested and compounded over time. This means you are always better off having "losses" than gains. Long-term capital gains are taxed at half the rate as short-term gains are, and the tax losses harvested from an investment portfolio could allow to have a separate trading portfolio tax-free. This "tax alpha" increases your after tax returns by up to 1.5 percent per year! It sounds complicated though doesn't it, like it might not be worth the time to do? That means it is a job for software!

Wealthfront has just this software, and for those who want to beat the market, they use every little trick in the book to beat the market. Since they are a robo-advisor, they don't charge much. They only charge 0.25 percent, which is about 25 percent of what a traditional advisor would charge. In my opinion, they are 100 percent worth it and will help you beat the market. They have some of the smartest people in finance working for them, and their white papers are absolute genius. They aren't paying me anything to plug them, I am just impressed with their stuff. If you want additional reading, I recommend going to their website and tooling around. Even if you don't use their service they publish great research for free.

Closing

Don't listen to the gurus who tell you that you can't beat the market. I just showed you several ways you can beat the market, and none of them are particularly complicated or fancy. You deserve to be rich if you are smart and work hard. My job is to help you make that happen.

I hope you enjoy my books as much as I enjoy writing them. For more, check out my other title on Amazon, "How to Make a Million Dollars Trading Options." It contains the contents of an email I received from a multimillionaire options trader. It is enlightening to say the least!

Until next time,
Cameron Lancaster

How to Make a Million Dollars Trading Options

Publishers Note: This was anonymously emailed to us from a successful trader who became disgruntled with Wall Street but didn't want his name publicly disclosed.

How to Make a Million Dollars Trading Options

Copyright © 2017, Lancaster Chatham Publishing

Anonymous Email: I'm a successful options trader. I work at (redacted) and I am (redacted) I can't talk about my total profits due to my confidentiality clauses in my contract, but suffice it to say I have made a lot of money trading for my clients. I see retail investors like you getting ripped off every day, and I would like to change that. The primary reasons that people lose money when trading options is that they don't know how to value assets (this gets worse the more complex the assets are), and their expenses are too high. I estimate that the public loses over a billion dollars annually attempting to trade options.

Understand The (Actual) Basics Of Options

When we use options:
1. **When I want big time leverage on a stock moving to the upside– I buy call options.**
2. **When I want to take advantage of heightened volatility in the market or make a bet on what price a stock will trade at expiration–I sell net credit spreads, almost always put spreads.**

Almost every other thing that you can do in the options market is designed by market makers to transfer your money into their pocket over time.

There are a million strategies you can use to try to make money in options. I think 95 percent of them are garbage. I will break down the expected returns of each option strategy later.

Options, simply put, are the right to buy or sell a stock. The right to buy is called a call option, and the right to sell is called a put option. The buyer pays an upfront premium in exchange for this right, and if the stock doesn't move the way they expect, they aren't forced to do anything, which is why they are called "options". All stock options have specified prices where you are permitted to buy or sell the stock; this is called the **strike price**. You have the choice of buying options to buy the stock below the current trading price- "in the money," at the current price-"at the money," or above the current price-"out of the money". The further out of the money the option is, the riskier the bet. Also, options are only good for so long, meaning they expire. The expiration date for equity options in the United States was traditionally after the market close on the third Friday of the month, but nowadays, the exchanges offer options that expire every single

Friday. This is the **expiration date** you see when you look up options on your online brokerage. Also, American call and put options trade in 100 share contracts, so if you buy one call option, it gives you the right to 100 shares. If you buy 20, that's 2000 shares. However, the quote you see on your online brokerage account is per share, so remember to multiply by 100!

People who buy options do so because they get an enormous amount of leverage for the money, *meaning if the stock moves a little, they make a lot of money.* People who sell options do so to collect the premiums. One of the biggest groups of options sellers are retired people who sell options on stocks they own to bring in steady income. Banks and stock trading firms sell a lot of options too, but typically use complex hedging techniques to ensure they make a profit no matter which way the market moves. My research indicates that sellers have a systematic advantage over buyers, but options sellers tend to make steadier profits punctuated by quick drawdowns, while options buyers tend to see more in the way of feast or famine returns. However, call options have high, positive returns, and are deadly in the hands of a skilled trader. I will break down the theory and show the advantages and disadvantages of each group later.

How do you trade options? You trade options the same way you trade stocks, go to your online brokerage account and usually next to where you input orders for stocks, you can input orders for options. You do usually need to fill out a form or two acknowledging the risks of trading options before you begin, but the process to get in to trading options is not that difficult. If you are a first time options trader, you usually get by default what is called a level 2 approval to buy calls and puts, and sell calls covered by stock positions (level 1). Level 3 approval is not too hard to get either, and it allows you to sell options, provided you have enough cash to cover the maximum loss or do a credit spread to hedge the risk.

If you believe that Apple is going to go higher and AAPL is trading for 135 dollars a share, you can buy a call option giving you the right to buy AAPL at 135 for 30 days. In this example, let's say your premium is 2 dollars per share and you buy 25 contracts. If AAPL rallies to 140, you can exercise the option to buy for 135 a share, and immediately sell for 140. Don't worry about not having the money to exercise an option; your broker will do it for you even if you don't have the money to buy the stock outright. Your profit in this case would be 3 dollars per share multiplied by the 2500 shares in the contract, pocketing you a cool 7500 dollars on a less than 5 percent move in the stock over a month. You just tripled your money! The benefit to buying call options on a stock is that your gain is theoretically unlimited. For example, if by some freak accident AAPL skyrockets to 150 per share, you wind up pocketing 32,500 dollars on your trade, and this happens often enough that you hear about it from other traders, usually when they put pictures of their new BMWs on Facebook. However, if AAPL sinks to 130, or even holds steady at 135, you lose your entire investment of 2500 dollars. However, one of the keys to success trading options is to not always hold them until the end of their expiration, as you will see in a little while. That way, if the stock doesn't move when you think it is going to, you can sell your option and get a good chunk of your money back if you don't wait until the expiration date. *Options are like milk; they're best for your health when they're not about to expire.* An important thing to note about options is that you can sell them at any time; you don't need to wait until the expiration to exercise them. *In fact, you should never exercise an option when you can sell instead.* There are theoretically times when you should exercise instead of selling, it usually happens with deep in the money options around dividend payout dates and stocks with wide bid/ask spreads on their options. In practice, the large number of arbitrageurs trading with complex software means that I have never been in a situation over my thousands of trades where I would have been better off by exercising. That situation will never happen in AAPL, although it might happen on a small stock with thinly traded options. You will find this to be true for you also. For example, if AAPL rallies to 137 in the first week, the option should be worth 3 dollars and change, but if you exercise, you lose the extra premium.

Anyway, you trade options the same way you trade stocks, through your online broker order entry screen, the only difference is that options have some different characteristics. These characteristics are known as the "Greeks". Each Greek can be derived with some not so simple math from the Black Scholes equation. No worries though, if you use an online brokerage that supports options trading, the computer will do the math for you to spit out the Greeks. There are 5 major Greeks, I tend to pay attention to 3 of them in my trading. The other two are Vega and Rho, give the terms a Google if you are interested, they apply more to strategies I don't employ. The first Greek is called Delta. *Delta is just the amount that the option goes up in value if the stock goes up a dollar per share.* Delta is expressed as a number from 0 to 1. Options that are really far in the money are going to have Deltas close to 1, meaning that if the stock moves up a dollar, so do the options. Options that are at the money will always have a Delta of roughly 0.5, meaning they go up about 50 cents for every dollar the stock moves. Options that are out of the money have Deltas closer to zero, because the stock has to move a long way for them to have any value. For example, if you buy 145 strike calls in AAPL when it is trading for 135, you might only get a 10 cent increase in the value of your options until it gets closer to the money. Note that Delta changes as the stock moves up and down. An option that is out of the money can become in the money if the stock moves up sharply, making the buyer of the option a lot of money in the process. *In the real world, Traders use Delta as a proxy for the probability that the stock will be at or above the strike price when the option expires.*

When the Delta changes on a stock due to the options going further in the money or further out of the money, this change is expressed as Gamma. Gamma is simply the rate that Delta changes. So, if the stock goes up a dollar per share, the delta will increase. Gamma is also measured as a decimal from 0 to 1. For normal trading, all you need to know is that the Delta will increase when the stock goes up, and will decrease if the stock goes down.

The third, and most important Greek, in my opinion, is Theta. In exchange for unlimited rewards on the upside of a stock, call buyers have to pay a premium to be able to buy the stock at a fixed price for a period of time. There are two parts to the value of an option, time premium, and intrinsic value. Time premium shrinks nearly every day, and at the end of the option, all that is left is the intrinsic value, meaning the option is in the money and the option has value due to the ability to sell or exercise for a profit. If the option is not in the money at the expiration, it has no intrinsic value. The time premium will also be valued at zero at expiration, so the option is *worthless.* Every day the stock doesn't go up, the value of the option suffers from **time decay**, which is expressed as Theta. Theta is written as a decimal and is the amount that the time premium of option will decay per day, regardless of whether the stock goes up or down. Theta works 24/7 to erode the value of call options. It works kind of like the event horizon of a black hole. One thing I notice from my trading is that time decay (Theta) seems to happen in chunks. If the stock holds steady for the day and the option isn't close to expiration, sometimes the option won't drop at all, but if the stock sells off the next day, the options will get absolutely crushed and lose even more time premium than you would expect. Theta can be your worst enemy or your best friend; it just depends on how you set up your strategies. If you sell options, you will be toasting to Theta all the time, and if you buy them, you will curse Theta on a daily basis.

The most time decay in the life of an option occurs in the last month of its existence before expiration. Notice what happens about a week out, the value of the option goes straight down like the option is falling into a black hole. This is where I like to sell out of the money put options, but so I don't want to risk losing massive amounts of money, I hedge the puts I sell with a put a ways further out of the money so I know the maximum loss I can sustain. This is important to do because of the black swan risk that is present in the market at all times, when selling puts, you are only one "flash crash" away from bankruptcy. I'm sure a few traders were bankrupted back in 2010 when the infamous "flash crash" scrubbed a trillion dollars in US market value in 36 minutes. So, limit your risk when you sell puts, just like insurance companies buy reinsurance, you should buy cheap puts so you can quantify your maximum loss but still take advantage of the positive expected value of your trade. The beauty of trading put spreads is that options get more expensive the more stocks go down, due to increased volatility, puts included. *This gives you an opportunity to make some cash every time the market has a decent correction.* If the market falls 10 percent, it doesn't become riskier in my opinion, I think it becomes less risky. I think you can make some nice cash by selling "insurance" by selling puts into market corrections, and covering your ass by buying a much further out of the money put. When you do this, it's called a credit spread, because you get cash deposited into your account when you make the trade, and when the option expires out of the money, you pocket 100 percent, free and clear.

I'm not a Nobel prize winning mathematician by any means, but I think it would stand to reason that you are better off holding options that have a month or two left to go if you want to be buying them, and if you want to sell options, you are better off taking advantage of that exponential rate of decline at the end of the graph by selling options with less than a month out. It is somewhat riskier to sell options closer to expiration, and it does decrease your upside to pay more premiums to buy a call option with a couple months to live, but that's my preferred way of trading options. I do not believe that the options market is fully efficient. I will explain why in a little while, and you are welcome to agree or disagree with me.

Understand Volatility and Put/Call Parity

The Greeks are the characteristics of how options move in relation to the stock, but how are they determined? Why is an option for AAPL at 135 worth 2 dollars a share for a month? Options get their value from volatility. Next to the Greeks on any options quote you see on your online brokerage is a number for **implied volatility.** Options are valued based on the underlying volatility of the stock, which is quoted as an annualized standard deviation. In plain English, the implied volatility is how much the market expects the stock to move over the next year, based on the price of the option. Again, you don't need to know advanced calculus to derive the implied volatility number; your computer will do it for you. You can readily compare the implied volatility with the **historical volatility** of the same stock, which is usually calculated as the volatility of the stock over the past 30 days. The historical volatility isn't always on the same screen, most brokers have a way to find the historical volatility, you just have to search around sometimes, and even if your broker doesn't have it, there are online services you can use. If you want to trade options seriously, you need this data. Etrade and Interactive Brokers both have the historical volatility as an option in their stock charts.

The thing is, implied volatility and historical volatility are usually different numbers. This can occur for a variety of reasons, such as an upcoming earnings announcement, a more volatile market, or bias on the part of traders. The interesting thing I have found in my research is that traders are consistently biased in their view of implied volatility. *In fact, over long periods of time, the average implied volatility is around 19 percent, whereas the average realized volatility of the options is only about 16 percent.* (Eraker, 2007, NYU Stern School of Business) This translates into large profits for sellers of options, especially put options, as you will see in a little while. So, if traders are consistently overvaluing options, we can systematically take advantage of their bias. Furthering this advantage is the fact that stocks tend to go up over time, favoring call buyers and put sellers. Puts and calls can't reflect the return of the underlying stock, because they are forced to trade at parity by arbitrage. This is called put/call parity.

The equation for this, in its simplest form, is that **Stock=Call-Put.** You can replicate a stock position of 100 shares, for example, by buying an at the money call, and selling a put, meaning you take the risk all the way to zero on the 100 shares stock, and you have unlimited upside on the 100 shares, and your options premiums will cancel each other out. If they didn't you could make free money by arbitrage, synthetically creating puts, calls or stock from buying and selling the other two. No matter how you rearrange this algebraically, it remains true. So if you want a call, it is the same thing as owning stock and buying a put to protect your downside. If you want a put, you need minus stock (short selling), and to buy a call. This may be difficult to do if you are a retail trader, but to Wall Street traders with 8 and 9 figure lines of credit, it could not be easier to synthetically arbitrage stocks and options. Why is this important that stocks and puts have to trade at parity? The reason why this is important is that the expected return for a put and a call are not the same, even if they are forced to trade at parity by arbitrage. The only factor that affects how puts and calls are valued is the volatility of the underlying stock, not the expected return. The expected return of stocks is positive, meaning put buyers collectively lose boatloads of cash, and call buyers collectively make boatloads of cash. It doesn't sound like it should be this simple, but it really is. *Calls really are just highly leveraged positions in appreciating assets. Puts, on the other hand, are insurance.* Insurance is meant to protect your assets against loss, not make you a profit. Therefore, institutional investors sometimes sell puts to protect their large stock positions from downside. Note that this doesn't kill their returns completely, just reduces their risk in exchange for peace of mind. The people who sell them insurance, on the other hand, make a profit on average, and a very good one if they control risk properly. Retail investors make mistakes when they trade options, focusing too much on buying puts, buying calls that are too far out of the money, and timing their trades poorly.

Know the Expected Value

of Options Contracts

The key to making money trading is being able to value the expected return of an asset better than the suckers you trade against, and if you do that, you make money. I said before that the way I like to trade options is to either use long call options as a proxy for stock, or use net credit spreads as to play volatility. But how do you select expirations, strikes, etc? Expiration is easy to select, just pick an expiration that gives you a little more time than you think you need, with a minimum of a couple weeks to go if you are buying, and a couple weeks or less if you are selling. Strike prices, on the other hand, is a little complicated, so we need to delve a little into options pricing theory to fully understand it. As I discussed in the put/call parity section, call options are basically a substitute for long stock, except with limited downside. **What I am going to prove to you is that the higher your strike price is, the higher your expected return is, and the higher your**

risk is also. This holds true all the way until the option is at the money, out of the money options are valued a little differently because a lot of people buy them as lottery tickets. So remember that **Stock=Call-Put?** If the strike equals zero, then you can't sell a put, since the right to sell a stock for zero is worthless. Therefore, stock is a call option with a strike price of zero. Your risk of loss is limited to your total investment, since stocks can't trade for negative amounts. Now, on AAPL, there are strikes all the way from 45 dollars per share in the current month all the way to 200 dollars a share. I went through the options chains to see the values for each option, and I had to go to the 130 strike before I found any options with a delta less than 99 cents per dollar. Time premium isn't really coming into play here at all until you hit the 125 strike. AAPL trades at about 136 at the time of writing this.

For example, on the 50-dollar strike, you are paying 86 dollars to per share to control a stock that is worth 136 dollars. You are getting some nice leverage for less than a 1 percent implied interest rate! On the 100-dollar strike, you pay about 36 dollars to control a 136-dollar stock, giving you roughly 4-1 leverage. The Delta is still 99.7, so you really are getting this leverage. On the 125 strike, you get a delta of around 97, and you have 13-1 leverage on the stock. Want to get the maximum bang for your buck on a 1-dollar move in the stock? In my experience, you get the most bang for your buck by buying the strike nearest to the stock price. The 135 strike here gives you about 40 to 1 leverage on AAPL. Calculate your **Delta** by multiplying the number of shares you get in your contract by the quoted Delta. Then divide by how much this cost you to get your **leverage** on the stock. You will theoretically make more money from out of the money options for large stock moves, but my research indicates that out of the money call options tend to be overvalued and have flat or negative expected returns. There are a lot of studies that have been done on the expected returns of options, which get some contradictory results, but I found one to be more helpful than the others. The study, done by two gentlemen named Coval and Shumway at the University of Michigan Business School found that call option returns increase as you go higher in the strike price, and that at the money calls return roughly a positive 2.5 percent per week on average. They also noted that while the absolute returns on call options are impressive (10-12 percent per month, on average), and over 100 percent per year, the risk adjusted returns kind of suck. They thought that for the risk, calls should return about 4 percent per week. This makes sense though, because of the incredible amount of leverage that call options give you trading stocks. How does this help you make money? It tells you 2 things.

1. Blindly buying call options isn't a good idea for the amount of risk that you take. Call options that are in the money or at the money do better than those that are out of the money.
2. Call options have huge returns, and equally huge risk.

By the way, here's what they found the returns were for buying puts. The average put return per week? Minus 6-7 percent!! Buying puts to place concentrated bets against stocks doesn't sound that dumb, but when you look at the numbers, you have a colossal wealth transfer happening on a daily basis due to people buying puts. Imagine if your car insurance cost 7 percent of your car's value per week. You would go bankrupt. Coval and Shumway point out that many people who buy puts do so to protect their long stock positions, but I personally suspect that there are a few townhouses in Manhattan paid for by retail traders buy puts on companies they hate. In this same vein, strategies like straddles are very poor investments. Inside the mind of an amateur trader "I don't know which way Apple will move after earnings, but I think it will move a lot," so I will buy both calls and puts. WRONG. You wouldn't go on a gambling spree before you go buy personal umbrella insurance, so don't buy puts and calls at the same time either. You can't afford to ignore the statistics of the markets if you want to be rich.

Call options, despite not having the best risk adjusted returns, are a deadly tool in the hands of a good trader. Since call option values are connected with the value of the underlying stock, anyone who can make good money trading stocks can make great money trading options.

How to Size Your Trades:

John Kelly vs. John Daly

One of the biggest questions in trading is how much capital to bet on each trade. There are a variety of methods, and I will give them each a grade based on how well I think they work.

The John Daly Method- **Grade–F** Most traders are gunslingers. They size their trades based on their convictions, and swing for the fences far too often. Their trading style reminds me of former professional golfer John Daly. I love John Daly's game, the man was very long off the tee, but I probably wouldn't give him my money to manage. Don't be the kind of trader who swings for the fences every time, betting 30-50 percent of your capital on each penny stock or options trade. If you swing for the fences every time, you end up risking losing all of your money. Having no plan is not having a trading plan.

The Martingale- **Grade–F** If you have ever been to a casino, you have seen someone do the Martingale. Basically, how the martingale works is every time you lose a bet (trade), you double the size of your bet (trade) until you make your money back. A martingale trader usually starts with betting like 5,000 per trade on a 100,000 dollar account and doubling down every time they lose. 95 percent of the time, it works and they run up your account balance to a little higher than you started, at which point the martingale trader usually withdraws the profit and goes on a spending spree. "What are the odds of losing 7 times in a row," they usually declare. They always end up broke, because some time in the course of their life, they do indeed lose 7 in a row or 8 in a row or whatever it takes to bankrupt them.

Fixed Amount- **Grade D+** A lot of traders like to bet a fixed amount on each trade, for example if they have a 50,000 dollar trading account, they bet a flat 5,000 on every trade. While not as exaggerated as the martingale, fixed amount betting runs into some of the same problems as the martingale, namely that it doesn't increase exposure when times are going well and decrease it when the account is vulnerable from drawdowns.

Fixed Fractional- **Grade C+** Fixed fractional traders will put, for example, 10 percent of their available capital in each trade, giving them protection from drawdowns and allowing them to benefit from rising markets by placing progressively more capital at play. The reason why this doesn't get an A is not all trading strategies are created equal, and traders can underbet on good strategies and overbet on bad strategies.

Full Kelly Criterion- **Grade A–** John Kelly was an engineer at AT&T in the 1950s who contributed to the field of advantage gambling and trading with his invention of the Kelly Criterion. The Kelly Criterion says to bet an amount of your capital equal to the positive expected value of the trade. For example, at the money call options have a positive expected value of 9 percent over a month, so the optimal amount of your capital to play at the money call options with is 9 percent or less. Note that the expected value of put options and far out of the money is actually negative, so the Kelly Criterion dictates that you should allocate zero dollars to them. Additionally, when using the Kelly Criterion to size trades, you can keep the rest of the money in a liquid mix of ETFs in an allocation like 85 percent bonds and 15 percent stocks, giving you an annual return averaging over 20 percent. You can make a living trading like that! The elegant part of the mathematics of

the Kelly Criterion is that
Kelly maximizes the logarithmic growth of your cash. Bet any more, and your capital grows less fast. Bet any less, and you leave some money on the table.

Play With the House's Money- **Grade A+** The Kelly Criterion (Fractional)- The best way to trade is to build on my earlier point about keeping the other 90 percent of your capital invested in less risky bets. One key point of modern portfolio theory is that you can invest in multiple risky assets, and collectively they are safer than any one individual bet. You don't have to bet the whole 9 percent on call options per month, in fact, you can bet less and your returns decrease more slowly than your risk decreases. To trade properly, set up two accounts, one for long-term investments, and one for trading. Put all your current money into a long-term investment account, but take the dividends and after tax capital gains and put them in your trading account. When you make new cash contributions to your account, do 70 percent into your long-term investment account, and put 30 percent into your trading account. This way, you are always playing with the house's money. Let the returns of your trading strategies drive your bet size, not the other way around! Do this, and you put yourself on the path to raking in the cash.

Where to Find Trading Ideas

1. The 52-week high list. I am always a fan of trading on momentum. Research shows that stocks at their 52 week highs tend to continue to go up. These are the Amazons, Googles and Apples of the world, and great companies tend to find themselves perpetually at the 52 week high. This tends to work best for stocks over 100 dollars a share–share prices send an important signal about the underlying company. How does a company trade for 900 dollars a

share, like Amazon does? The do it by being damn successful! Stocks end up at 5 dollars a share because they lose money. Stocks end up in the triple digits because they make money. Plain and simple.

2. Short Selling firms. I'm not really a fan of shorting stocks, I don't think it tends to be profitable, but there are research firms that publish about stocks they think are overvalued or straight up fraudulent. The most notable of these firms is Citron Research. I've been on both sides of Citron's calls, and they have made me a lot of money when I have been on their side and lost me money when they called against me. You don't have to trade in the same direction as Citron or any other notable short selling firms, but you should understand that they move the market. Follow them on twitter, and they'll send you calls in real time.

3. StockTwits. Ever hung out at a craps table? Stocktwits is the online trading version of a craps table. Go to front page of Stocktwits and they have a section for trending stocks. These are the most talked about, and therefore traded stocks of the day. See what other people are saying, form your own opinion, and fire away. You already know that long options are the way to go, so when you see stocks moving up on stocktwits to a lot of chatter, buy them, sell them a few hours later, and profit.

Why Most Options Traders Lose Money

Trading is a business. If you go long stocks or their derivatives, you should make money over time. This is the market rewarding you for taking risk (*beta*). If you beat other traders over time, this adds an additional component to your profit (*alpha*). Your gross profit is equal to your alpha plus your beta. That is your gross profit. Your expenses are your commissions, fees, bid/ask spreads, and margin interest. The dirty little secret about trading is that most traders make money before expenses, and lose money after expenses. This is a business, not a game. Here's what you can do about each expense.

- Commissions- Use Robin Hood or Interactive Brokers. As of writing this, I don't think you can do options on Robin Hood, but they are free for stocks. Interactive Brokers is 1 dollar per trade, vs Etrade which charges 6.95. By not using a retail oriented broker like Etrade or Scottrade you cut your commission cost 85 plus percent. Do you want to make money or lose money? Pay attention to your damn expenses! 80 percent of retail traders are at firms that charge over 5 dollars in commission. Wall Street nibbles away at your cash, getting rich off you and transferring your money into their pocket, 7 bucks at a time.

- Fees- This mainly applies to longer term investors who pay people to manage their money for them. If you are paying any fees, you need to be able to justify them, just like if you were running a business.
- Bid/Ask spreads- Do you have 1 million dollars in stock you need to take liquidity for to sell? If not, why are you using market

orders? This is a Wall Street scam. In business, the person who makes the offer typically gets a better price. Case in point, car dealers offer cars for sale, and buy them cheap at auction. They always name their price. Who doesn't name their price? Dumb consumers who want a brand new car and don't like negotiating. Business requires you to negotiate, use limit orders for your inventory.

- Margin Interest- If you are paying 9 plus percent to borrow stocks when Interactive Brokers charges 2 percent, you are an idiot. That's fine though, there is still time to switch to a broker that charges a better rate for margin. Etrade charges like 10 percent on margin, that's what the expected return of most stocks is. So the customer takes 100 percent of the risk, and Etrade gets 10 percent, risk free... Genius for Etrade, horribly stupid for anyone who borrows from them.

Bonus Tips on Trading

- When you set limit orders to buy or sell, set them at random prices, not at round numbers. For example, set your order for 99.98 instead of 100, because lots of institutional traders are lazy and call in round numbers to their brokers.
- Large Bid/Ask spreads can either represent opportunity or trouble for options traders. You don't want to trade contracts that aren't liquid, but if, for example, the bid is for 0.90 and the ask is for 1.05 on an option, I would try to buy for 0.90 and sell for 1.05. You just have to be patient and move the limit around if it doesn't work in the first 20 minutes or so. Volatility can be your friend as much as your enemy, Benjamin Graham and Warren Buffett would agree.

- Patience is key, every 9-12 months you typically see a 9-10 percent pullback in stocks. Corrections are guaranteed to happen, don't stress out of the market is too calm. Go play golf instead or take time off to travel if the market is slow. The market as a whole tends to be really slow from mid July to mid August, that is an excellent time of year to take a break from trading for you also. If half of Wall Street is frolicking in the Hamptons, you should do something similar. Emulate the successful, trading isn't the kind of job where you make money for showing up every day. It is more important to not be wrong than to be right.
- For your first trade of the quarter or your first trade with a new deposit, do something high percentage to put a win on the board. Selling out of the money weekly puts works well for this. It is so much easier to make money with a positive attitude and

nothing inspires a positive attitude like playing with the house's money.

The public loses billions trading options, and the only people who know why won't tell the public. *Approach trading like a business and you are well on your way to making money. Approach it like entertainment, and you will get what you pay for. Expected value is everything, do the math and follow the money. Nothing can make you more money than smart speculation, and sometimes all it takes is a couple good options trades in a row. That's what worked for me.*

Until Next Time,
Cameron Lancaster

The Passive Income Playbook: How Alternative Investments Can Help You Get Rich and Retire Early

The Passive Income Playbook: How Alternative Investments Can Help You Get Rich and Retire Early

Copyright ©2017 Lancaster Chatham Publishing

What if you could get higher returns for lower risk? Would you take it? The stock market is great for growing your capital over the long term, but it isn't the only game in town. Many, many millionaires have been made with smart investments in real estate, private businesses, and other alterative investments. This book is about showing you how to take advantage of each of these opportunities, which can supplement or replace stock market investing and make you rich. Passive income has life changing benefits for those who earn it, and you can do much better than dividend paying stocks when it comes to passive income. So if passive income is your goal, you need to look at alternatives to a traditional stock and bond portfolio.

Inside:

- How you can get started investing in real estate, the world's first great creator of wealth, even if you don't have a big down payment.
- How peer-to-peer investment platforms change the investing game, giving you access to consumer loans, real estate partnerships, and hard money loans.
- How real estate can reduce your taxes.
- How you can refinance your properties to buy even more property, effectively cloning your investments.
- How to select businesses that you can buy and run semi-absentee, giving you round the clock income, and more.

You can get rich, retire early, dump the 9-5, and live the life you want. What you need is some real world education on how alternative investing works, and how to get rich.

Is the Stock Market the Best Place to Invest?

The media tells you that if you have some extra money to invest, the best place to put that money is in the stock market. After all, that's how Warren Buffett got rich, right? As anyone who had money in the market during the 2008 financial crisis can attest, the stock market is not a smooth ride all the time. Stocks fell over 50 percent peak to trough, and a lot of investors panicked and sold.

A lot more people than you think panicked and sold during the fall of 2008 leading into the bottom of that market in March 2009. I feel for them. Nobody should have to work their whole life, saving up money and doing everything right, only to lose it all with one bad decision to sell at the bottom of a catastrophic bear market. I think everyone knows someone who has lost some money in the stock market. The stories go like this, "My friend lost 100k investing in their friend's biotech company, or so and so bought into a hot technology stock that ended up being on the wrong side of the market." Usually in these stories there is some element of doubling down involved, often after an investment has gone sour, people double down, investing money they really can't afford to lose in a bad stock. I'm here to tell you that if you know someone who has lost money in the market, or are close with someone who has, forgive them, or forgive yourself if you were the one who lost.

The market is a psychological roller coaster, and the truth is that many people have a difficult time making money in the stock market. **In fact, the stock market can be psychological hell.** Personally, I am a person who is very logical, and I'm in a good place financially, so I like the stock market, and fully understand that it goes down sometimes but the risk justifies the reward. I also like alternatives to the stock market, because I like to have multiple income streams and I like to hedge my bets. When you invest in different assets that aren't correlated with each other, you greatly increase the chance of making money in any given year, month, week or day.

The stock market might not be for you if:

- **You have a tendency to panic when the market falls sharply**, which it does do on average every 5-7 years. The stock market is a profitable investment for most people.

If you have lost money in stocks over more than a 3-4 year period, the stock market probably isn't for you.

- **You like to take a more hands-on role in your investments.** The fact is that the management and employees of large corporations soak up a large portion of the profits for themselves. If you don't mind doing some of the legwork yourself, enjoy working with others, and want control over your money, than you probably would be better off looking at alternatives to stocks.

- **You want more leverage than stocks allow.** The stock market and borrowed money are not a good combination for everyone. However, most people are familiar with how mortgages work, and how business loans work. The fact is that you can get a lot more long term leverage investing in private businesses or real estate than you can in stocks.

Even if you have the kind of personality well suited to the stock market, you can improve your returns and lower your risk by diversifying into other investments, as you will see.

The Wide World of Investments

Where else can you put your money besides the stock market? Under your mattress is the first thought for many people when they have extra money, but putting money under the mattress doesn't earn any return. The best places besides stocks to put your money, in my opinion, are:

- **Real estate.** Where do you think the government wants you to invest? If you look at their policies, I would say that the government wants you to invest in real estate. If you can afford it, you want to own your own home. The reason why is that when you rent, the money that you pay goes towards paying off someone else's mortgage. Your landlord can and will raise the rent on you whenever they are between contracts, because they own the place and you don't. Just like sometimes the smartest investment move you can make is to pay off high interest debt, they first step to getting in on the real estate game is to own your own housing. It's much better, financially speaking, to "rent" from a bank via a mortgage than rent from a landlord via rent. However, if you want to make passive income investing in real estate, you need cash flow. Renting your property out is how you get passive income machine to start working in your favor. Real estate is THE place to look if you want to get consistent double-digit returns.

- **Peer to Peer Investments-** Websites like Prosper, Lending Club, Realty Shares, and PeerStreet allow you invest in loans and real estate projects with much less money than you would need otherwise. Instead of needing tens or hundreds of thousands of dollars to get started, you can get started with as little as a few hundred to a few thousand. Lending Club and Prosper allow small investors to make loans to other consumers via crowdfunding. Realty Shares, and PeerStreet allow small investors to get in on a pipeline of real estate deals that traditionally have had six figure minimum investments. This new crowd funded model makes it possible for small investors to get access to high return real estate deals or loans, and also allows developers in need of capital to quickly get funding. This is a win-win for both sides, and is truly a disruptive business model to the status quo. The best part about this for you is that the returns are high, safe, and predictable. We will cover each one of these platforms later in detail.

- **Semi-absentee businesses.** Those of you who run a more time intensive business may groan when you read this, but semi-absentee businesses have made more millionaires by the truckload. There are really two kinds of businesses in this world. The first kind is the kind that needs a sharp owner to be CEO, coach, and quarterback. The other kind is the kind that can be run by an 18-year old kid, because, well, that's your demographic for minimum wage retail jobs. Examples of businesses that need a great quarterback are bars, restaurants, car dealerships, and anything with a lot of inventory. These are also the businesses that everyone cautions you against starting because they tend to take over your life. If you want a business that you can pay someone to run while you enjoy the profits, you need to follow a few criteria. Businesses that have a license they can lose easily (liquor stores), are inventory intensive (restaurants and car dealers come to mind), or have lots of receivables (anything manufacturing) are not passive or semi-passive businesses. You want businesses that make money while you sleep, or you can pay someone else to run without too much risk of them destroying it. Good examples of semi-absentee businesses are car washes, laundromats, real estate with a property manager, authority websites, book publishing ;), and similar businesses.

These are all good examples of places you can invest your money without the constant drama of having your assets marked to market on your brokerage screen. If passive income is your goal, these investments are your solution.

Real Estate

Real estate is the oldest means of getting rich in the world. Back in roman times, landlords owned big blocks of tenements (apartments), rented them out, used the money to build more, and became some of the richest people in the empire. The reason? Everyone needs a place to live. They didn't have Fannie Mae or Bank of America back then, but people invested in real estate and got rich. What has changed in the last 2,000 years in real estate? Not much, except maybe the apartments look different. Real estate is a great investment. Residential real estate pretty much went straight up in value from 1970 to 2007, when the housing bubble popped. Real estate is nowhere near being in a bubble in 2017, except maybe in San Francisco and the Bay Area. Bottom line, stocks are much more volatile than real estate.

Investing in real estate has steadier returns than stocks, which means two things to you. First off, you are allowed to use a higher amount of leverage when you buy real estate. Instead of putting 50 percent down on stocks like you would if you bought on margin, or 100 percent if you pay cash, you can put 10-25 percent down on real estate purchases, depending on what you bank requires. If you qualify for an FHA loan, you can put as little as 3.5 down, giving you an amazing 28 times leverage on your investment. If you qualify for a VA loan, you can put 0 percent down, and only have to pay a loan fee of a couple percent or so.

You don't have to have perfect credit score to get an FHA loan either. Even if your score is around 600 you can get a loan from the FHA. You have to meet certain requirements, such as having the payment be less than 30-35 percent of your income, and actually occupying the house, but if your finances are in order, you basically just have to sign on the dotted line and be able to make the payments. For example, if you are able to make 70,000 dollars per year and have a 11,000 dollar down payment, you can buy a 300,000 dollar house with an FHA loan. That right there is the American dream. Owning your own home has a benefit to you also in that it functions as somewhat of a forced savings plan, as each month, a fraction of your payment goes towards shrinking your mortgage. If you ever want to move, you will have your down payment and more waiting for you in home equity.

Your mortgage will only shrink if you make your payments, it will never get bigger. **Your property, on the other hand will appreciate in value by 2-4 percent per year on average, increasing your equity when you sell.** Real estate ownership is the key to going from middle class to being considered wealthy.

Where things start to get interesting is when you use an FHA loan to acquire a multi unit property. FHA loans are allowed for not only single-family homes, but also for duplexes, triplexes, and fourplexes. A potentially very savvy move if you are young and have a decent income is to buy a property with 3-4 units, live in one and rent out the other units. If you do it right, i.e. by buying a property below market and improving the value so that you can rent it for more, the other 2-3 people will pay your mortgage and put a little money in your pocket, and you get to live for free. The FHA lets you count some of your income from renting the property to help you qualify for these types of loans. The game plan is to buy a property, fix it up, rent it out, and cash in big on the appreciation, rent, and mortgage amortization. Then, when you want to move, you refinance the property using the income from the property, and you own an investment property and you can buy another home for yourself. As you continue to save money, you will be able to buy more property using the income that you already have from your main sources of income, such as your job, and your investment income, which comes from your properties.

You can actually clone your properties by refinancing them, cashing out, and using the money for down payments on other properties. Since you are allowed to put less than 10-20 percent down, and since real estate is cash flow positive, if you do it right, you can make a lot of money in a hurry.

Investing in real estate is an excellent way to build wealth, because your return comes from four different components. The four components of your return are:

1. Rent. When you own real estate that you don't need to occupy, you can rent it out. As long as the rent you receive is greater than your mortgage and expenses, you have a cash flow positive property. Your mortgage will never grow if you make the payments, and your expenses should be easy to budget for as long as you don't ignore them, so you should be able to easily turn a profit on property that you own. The numbers back this up, and as of 2017, it is cheaper to own a property than to rent in 42 states out of 50. Even if you think your market is cheaper to rent than own you can still find property below market that you can improve the value of by making renovations, so you should be able to turn a profit regardless. Also, you need to consider the fact that rents rise over time, whereas mortgages stay fixed. So, over time, it will be cheaper to own in all 50 states based on normal rent growth patterns. The profit

that you will earn from renting real estate is expressed as your capitalization rate. Capitalization rates, or cap rates for short, are simply the rent divided by how much the property is worth. For example, if a property is worth a million dollars and rents for 75,000 dollars gross and clears 50,000 after repairs, property taxes and insurance, your cap rate is 5 percent. If your mortgage rate is 3.75 percent, then you are paying your mortgage and putting money in your pocket every month. That is a good deal for you! Cap rates tend to be higher for riskier properties, so be careful, but generally you want to see cap rates that cover your mortgage, plus a 20-25 percent margin of safety. You never want to own a property that takes more money to carry than you earn, that is how you end up broke. Real estate is harder to screw up than stocks, but you need to run the numbers and make sure that your investment is safe and has enough margin to pay your mortgage.

2. Property Appreciation. This is how you make the big money in real estate, but you don't necessarily want to rely on appreciation to make a profit on any given deal. Cash flow is the cake, but appreciation is the icing. If you own this same million-dollar property for 5 years and it appreciates at 3 percent compounded annually, you should be able to sell for 1,159,000 dollars, netting you a capital gain of 159k over that 5-year period. If you look back to the earlier graph, you will see that this is a likely outcome if you own good real estate. You never want to rely on it, but there is a 95+ percent chance that you will be able to sell for more than you bought for if you wait long enough. Property appreciation can also depend on where you are. If your market is hot, like parts of Texas and Colorado are in 2017, then you

are likely to experience property appreciation. If you are buying real estate somewhere with a perpetually weak economy, like Ohio or Michigan, then you need to make sure that your cash flow provides you enough return, because real estate tends to appreciate much more in hot economies.

3. Mortgage amortization. Every time you pay your mortgage, a little money is subtracted from your balance that you owe. Over time, as your mortgage shrinks, you own more and more equity in your property. This obviously means that you will net more on the sale after you pay off the loan. Property appreciation pulls your equity up, and paying down the mortgage pulls the amount that you owe down. Your net worth increases like clockwork, and you end up a winner. Also, if interest rates fall, you can refinance your mortgage and pay a lower interest rate, further improving your cash

flow. There are so many ways to win in real estate that it isn't even funny. In the stock market, there are so many negative possibilities coming at you from all over the world, in real estate you have a much higher degree of control. It really doesn't take a ton of skill to buy property and hold it as long as your rent exceeds your mortgage you end up a winner. If you have skill in renovation, you can increase the value of your property much more, but you too will benefit from the gentle push that mortgage amortization gives you.

4. Paper Write Offs. In the real world, you can't just claim nonexistent expenses and take a write off for them. Fortunately, real estate is not the real world as far as the US government is concerned. If you own residential property, which is what we are discussing, you can take a write off for the total value of your buildings (not the land though) over 27.5 years. Assuming the

value of the land is about 20 percent of the total value, which is typical of most markets, you can take a paper loss on your taxes for about 30,000 dollars per year, for 27.5 years. Does this mean that you can't deduct the cost of repairs? Hell no, this just is Uncle Sam thanking you for investing in real estate by not making you pay taxes. If your cap rate is 6 percent and your mortgage interest is 4 percent, and you have 20 percent equity in your property, then the way the math works out is that you end up with a profit of about 30,000 dollars in terms of cash flow, and you end up with a loss of about 2,000 dollars for tax purposes. The government does recapture the depreciation when you sell, but they give you a great loophole so that you can avoid paying taxes altogether.

Real estate is truly a gold mine when it comes to reducing your taxes. If you cash out a property and want to buy another one, you can use a 1031 exchange (google it) to buy another property of equal or greater value, and avoid paying taxes on the sale. This won't work for every situation, but it will work for most, and the 1031 exchange is a valuable thing to have in your toolbox as a real estate investor. Why? Because Uncle Sam likes you, that's why!

If you want to get started investing in real estate, you need to find properties to buy. You can find properties either on the MLS, which a real estate agent can help you do, you can buy properties at auction, or you can buy directly from interested owners. I would recommend that you buy properties that have either just come on the MLS very recently, or buy at auction. The reason why is that if a property has a good return, usually someone will try to buy it. If no one has tried to buy it, then it probably isn't a good deal. Alternatively, you can offer low prices at either an auction or to properties on the MLS, but you need to be prepared for the vast majority of your offers to be rejected. If they aren't, however, you know you are getting a good deal! Negotiation is paramount to your real estate investment success, as is keeping fees low. You want to brush up on the art of negotiation when you start your real estate journey.

Investing in real estate is a fantastic way to build wealth, but if you don't have enough money to get in yet, there is still hope. You can invest in real estate with much less money than you otherwise could by using peer-to-peer platforms, and you also can get access to lucrative markets such as credit card and debt consolidation loans too!

Peer to Peer Investment

Let's say you want to benefit from investing in real estate but you don't yet have the money you need to buy a place as an investment property yet. If it were 10 years ago, you would just have to wait until you had saved up enough money and had a long enough credit history to buy an investment property. Now, things are different. Peer to peer investing platforms make it much easier to invest in real estate, consumer loans, and really anything that has a high minimum investment. You might not have 50k for a down payment on a place, but if you had 10 friends each with 5,000 you could buy the place together, at least in theory. In practice, P2P platforms like Realty Shares and Peer Street work like having a bunch of friends who also invest in real estate. You don't know them, you don't work with them, but your capital is pooled with theirs when you invest in a project you like. What P2P investing can really do for you is to open up a whole world of alternative investments that you couldn't access otherwise with double-digit returns.

P2P investing is unique because it gives you more control over the investments that you choose than the stock market. For example, when you sign up for *Realty Shares*, a leading P2P investment platform, you are presented with a pipeline of real estate deals that you can invest in. You can choose to invest in hard money loans, which are loans secured by the real estate, or you can participate in the projects themselves. Everything is presented to you in the due diligence process, and you can see a great deal about the property, which you can use to determine whether you want to invest. Before the investments even get to you, they have to pass through Realty Shares' own due diligence process, which disqualifies a lot of obviously bad investments. The minimum investment currently is 5,000 dollars, which compared to other real estate projects is a low entry point. These kinds of investments have always existed, but until now, they had six figure minimum investments and were run by private equity people. The returns are really good. The hard money loans are returning from 8 to 12 percent, and the equity projects are returning 11-18 percent. If these numbers sound high, it's because you aren't used to doing private investments. Skilled managers are capable of hitting 18 percent more often than not with a little leverage involved. Of course, all the leverage is nonrecourse, so you can't lose more than you put in initially, and depending on the project, you should see some cash back starting about 6-12 months after you invest in a joint venture deal and from 1-6 months after you loan money in a hard money deal. 99+ of investments in these platforms are making money; the only downside is you're your money is tied up in the meantime. The point is that the biggest weakness of the stock market is also its biggest strength. **When you invest in real estate, one of the downsides is that you can't liquidate**

quickly. However, not being able to liquidate quickly is also the biggest strengths of real estate investing. It makes it significantly harder to make bad decisions. Instead of the volatile graph of the stock market, Realty Shares investments tend to look more like a straight line. If you invest in hard money loans, the developers make a substantial down payment, and have to pay the interest on time according to the schedule, often on a monthly basis. If they don't pay, you and the other lenders simply take the keys, change the locks and sell the property to someone else for a discount. Realty Shares handles that part for you, and your realistic worst-case scenario is simply that it takes longer to get your money back than you expected.

Peer Street is a lot like Realty Shares, except that the only investments on the platform currently are loans. They have a solid pipeline of projects coming in, and when combined with Realty Shares, should provide enough of pipeline for new investment cash at any given time. Peer Street has a very strong track record of investment success. There are other real estate peer to peer investment platforms but I recommend these two for a few reasons. They are:

- Bankruptcy remote structure. In the freak event that the platforms you invest in go bankrupt, your investments are held separately in a different company that has the sole purpose of holding loans. Some commentators have raised concerns that if peer-to-peer platforms are run poorly and go bankrupt, you investments will be unaffected. I don't worry a ton about this, but it defeats the purpose of peace of mind when you know that if your platform is bad at managing their money that they could be risking your investment too to the whims of bankruptcy court. The reason why this is an issue is because legally, you don't have a contract with the underlying investors, you have a contract with your platform. Every one of the platforms I recommend to you have this structure in place, except for lending club, which doesn't have one because it made it harder for them to get approved in all 50 states. However, lending club is the biggest player in the industry and has over a billion dollars in assets, as well as a backup-servicing plan, so I view it as a nonissue. It is something to consider nonetheless.

- Track record. Each one of these platforms has at least a couple years you can base data off of, which is important in this business. For example, banks require you to have a year or two of income you can prove so they see you can pay your mortgage. We should do the same with our investments.

You can also use peer to peer lending to invest in consumer loans through **Lending Club** and **Prosper**. Consumers refinance their credit card loans and auto loans, among other loans, through lending club, which allows people like you and I to fund the loans, with a minimum investment of 25 dollars. The returns tend to be in the 8-12 percent range if you do it right. The borrowers tend to be affluent, tech savvy, and carry a decent amount of consumer debt. In the Millionaire Trader series, there is a big section on lending club in *High Finance* by my colleague Logan C. Kane where he breaks down how robo advisors can improve returns in P2P lending. Lending Club is the biggest player in P2P, and they originate billions of dollars in loans, which they sell partially to Wall Street banks but also to ordinary investors through crowd funding. Prosper is like Lending Club's little brother, and they deal with a lot of borrowers who Lending Club might not approve, but are still considered to have good credit. Prosper has a bankruptcy remote structure, which is a big plus for peace of mind, whereas Lending Club does not. The main advantage of using LC over Prosper is that there is a secondary market for loans on LC, which gives you the means to sell most of your loans within a few weeks or so. If I only picked one between the two I would probably choose Prosper due to the greater peace of mind of the bankruptcy remote structure.

Lending Club and Prosper loans are for 3 or 5 year terms, and the borrowers pay monthly, paying you interest and principal every month that you can reinvest. You can invest in A+ credit borrowers all the way down to people at the edge of prime credit (640 FICO), some of them paying over 30 percent interest. Some will default, but if you diversify you should turn a really nice profit. It is really easy to diversify since the minimum investment is 25 dollars. If you invest in either LC or Prosper you should try to invest in at least 200 loans. This is a minimum investment of roughly 5,000 dollars either way. This makes it worthwhile to invest, and gives you a big enough sample size to see how you are doing.

P2P lending is a hot new trend that can deliver big returns to savvy investors, and I recommend playing it through Realty Shares, Peer Street, and Prosper. Lending Club is too big to ignore, and I encourage you to look at them too, even though I don't wholeheartedly recommend them. P2P lending can help you get some strong passive income, which you can use to take your financial life to the next level.

Semi-Absentee Businesses

I don't know about you, but I like the idea of being on vacation, drinking Coronas on the beach while I have a business open somewhere making me money to pay for my vacation. The right kind of business, run the right way, can provide a great potential for passive income and a high return. However, most business owners fail miserably at this task, because they choose the wrong kind of business. You can make a killing opening up a nice Italian restaurant with legitimately good food and a killer wine list, but when you own that kind of business, the business owns you. Now, you could have an awesome manager who takes care of things while you are away, but you need to have a profitable business to be able to pay the awesome manager the money he wants. If you don't have that, you are trapped. Also, many businesses are absolute minefields, with traps waiting for you in cash flow, inventory, receivables, and employee theft. What you need if you want passive income is the kind of business that is simple and easy to run, so you don't have to pay anyone else to do it. **This is called a semi-absentee business.** It is a fact that semi-absentee businesses fail at a much higher rate than manager owned businesses, but that is almost always because the business is too tricky for the management to handle, and the business has the wrong model for the owner and manager.

Characteristics of good semi-absentee businesses:

- Not a lot of inventory. Inventory is money, except you can't spend it, and until it moves, you don't' have money. If you own a restaurant, your inventory literally spoils if it isn't used. Not good. If you own a car dealership, you have millions of dollars of cars on the lot, and if you overpay for them, can't sell them, or have issues with your financier, you are out of business. Not good. Inventory makes it easy to screw up. On the other hand, if you own a business like a car wash, you don't have any inventory, unless you want to count soap. Other good businesses that can be run this way are auto repair places and laundromats. The common theme here is businesses that require equipment rather than inventory. This makes it much easier for you to be semi-passive.

- Not a lot of receivables. This applies especially to service businesses that tend to invoice on a 30-60 day schedule. If you own a business like this, you will spend a significant amount of time chasing down money from various people. This really kills the passivity part.
- Not highly regulated. Highly regulated industries, such as finance and insurance tend to have a lot of correspondence that needs to be responded to on a timely basis.

Businesses like these need a sharp person to quarterback the operation, deal with regulators, red tape, employees, etc. Regulation makes your life hard, the less of it you have to deal with, the better.

You want to be able to focus on the strategy of your business, not the day-to-day tactics. Your goals as a semi-passive business owner are marketing, driving traffic, managing expenses, and ensuring that the people you have working for you are intelligent and trustworthy people. You can make a ton of money with the right business, but beware of businesses that people say are turnkey. Also, think very carefully and do plenty of due diligence before entering into a business, because you can't always pivot away from a business quickly just because things aren't working the way you thought. That said, here's a list of good businesses you can run semi-absentee, giving you a solid passive income, plus a short explanation of each. They are listed from most passive to least passive.

Publishing/Creating Art- Passivity grade A+ Nothing is more passive than creating art once, which sells over and over again. Musicians, actors, artists, writers, at least those who are successful, work once and get paid 100 times. That is as good as it gets from a passive income standpoint. Your copyright is for life in the US, plus 70 years. I will get paid from this book for the rest of my life. I like that! Another plus is that the startup cost is very minimal, as in 3 figures max.

Internet- Passivity grade A. Affiliate marketing, blogging, and similar businesses can be a huge moneymaker if you have skills in that area. Same as publishing, creation of art, startup cost is very low. You can make a website for free and start driving traffic to it within minutes, which you can monetize with AdSense, Amazon Associates, et cetera. Once you get it going, traffic tends to keep flowing, as does your cash flow.

Lending Money- Passivity grade A. The stock and bond markets would also score a 9 on this, but P2P gives you more control over your investments, which actually increases your passive income potential. You can also find other sources of people who want to borrow money and lend to them.

Real Estate- Passivity grade A if you have no mortgage, B+ if you have a mortgage. Real estate is as passive as a physical business can be if you have a good property manager who deals with tenants, collects rent, etc. Paying a mortgage puts a little more pressure on you, but it's still a pretty passive investment.

Car Washes and Laundromats- Passivity grade B+. As long as you have a good location and 2-3 employees who show up to work when they say they are going to you have a very passive business that can make upwards of 30-40k a month in the right location.

Vending Machines- Passivity grade B. Refill vending machines, get cash, repeat. It works even better if you have enough of them that you can hire other people to stock them for you, if you could take advantage of scale, then I would give it a B+.

Auto repair- Passivity grade B-. I'm including this one because of the high profit potential and the chances of getting a good manager/mechanic who you could split profits with. Auto repair places are fairly capital intensive, but good businesses nonetheless.

Franchises- Passivity grade C+. Your mileage is going to vary on this but some franchises are very good investments.

This isn't an exhaustive list of businesses with passive income potential, but it is a fantastic start. You now have 3 great sources of passive income that don't involve the stock market and have high returns. Your sources of great investments are real estate, P2P investments, and semi-absentee businesses. You may not agree with everything I write, but hopefully I helped you think a little outside the box when it comes to your money. I hope you enjoyed reading this book as much as I enjoyed writing it.

In this book, you learned:
- How you can get started in real estate, the world's first great creator of wealth.

- How peer-to-peer investment platforms change the investing game, giving you access to consumer loans, real estate partnerships, and hard money loans.
- How real estate can shelter your income from taxes.
- How to select businesses that you can buy and run semi-absentee, giving you round the clock income.

Closing Thoughts- The Millionaire Trader Compilation

Whichever approach you choose, you are miles ahead of the majority of investors, who simply wing their investments and have no idea about expected value or the true wealth transfers that happen with investments in general. By placing yourself on the right side of the wealth transfer equation, you tee yourself up to increase your wealth and improve your family's future. Each book in this series offers a different angle on leverage, control, and passivity that align with different personalities of investors.

You should choose the style of investment that best suits your personality, whether it is actively trading, passively investing in stocks, real estate, or private business, matching your lifestyle and personality to your investments will go a long way to guarantee your success.

All the best,
Cameron Lancaster

www.ingramcontent.com/pod-product-compliance
Lightning Source LLC
Chambersburg PA
CBHW020914180526
45163CB00007B/2731